this book belongs to:

Anna
vejtasa

TOP 50 DEADLIEST CREATURES

Camilla de la Bédoyère

QEB

Created for QEB Publishing by Tall Tree Ltd
www.talltreebooks.co.uk
Editors: Jon Richards and Rob Colson
Designer: Jonathan Vipond
Illustration pp18–19:
Mick Posen/www.the-art-agency.co.uk

Published in the United States by
QEB Publishing, Inc.
3 Wrigley, Suite A
Irvine, CA 92618

www.qed-publishing.co.uk

A CIP record for this book is available from the
Library of Congress.

ISBN 978 1 78171 075 3

Printed in China

Picture credits
(t=top, b=bottom, l=left, r=right, c=center, fc=front cover,
bc=back cover)
Alamy: 8-9 Stephen Frink Collection, 20-21 Mark Conlin, 21br David
Fleetham, 26-27 Gerry Pearce, 30 blickwinkel, 30-31 Amazon-images, 2bl
William Mullins, 48-49 Wildlife GmbH, 74-75 Alaska Stock, 86-87 Phil
Degginger, 91t Allstar Picture Library, 94-95 Naturepix, 104b
WaterFrame,110-111 David Fleetham; **Corbis:** 49 DLILLC, 61t Tom
Brakefield, 61b Theo Allofs, 66-67 W Perry Conway, 72 Thomas Kitchin &
Victoria Hurst/All Canada Photos, 106-107 ML Sinibaldi; **Creative
Commons:** 44bl Bjorn Christian Torrissen.
Dreamstime: 50bl Yaireibovich; **FLPA** 17tr Malcolm Schuyl, 39t D P
Wilson, 42-43 Thomas Marent, 43t Thomas Marent, 51br Peter Davey,
70bl Piotr Naskrecki, 70-71 Chien Lee, 78-79 Norbert Wu/Minden
Pictures, 81b Reinhard Dirscherl, 80-81 Norbert Wu/Minden Pictures,
84bl Hiroya Minakuchi/Minden Pictures, 96-97 Pete Oxford/Minden
Pictures ,114 Mike Parry/Minden Pictures
Getty Images: 12 Visuals Unlimited, 23 Mark Moffett, Inc./Michael Kern,
40 Mark Moffett, 41r Visuals Unlimited, Inc/Alex Wild, 60 Vivek
Sinha,64-65 Pete Oxford, 72-73 Robert Postma, 74bl Daniel J Cox, 75br
Altrendo Nature, 86bl James H Robinson, 95t Dorling Kindersley,
110-111 AFP; **Minibeast Wildlife:** 82bl Alan Henderson; **Nature Picture
Library:** 4-5 Alex Mustard, 6b Alan James, 13t Michael D Kern, 16-17 Joe
McDonald, 17b Doug Perrine, 18-19 Doug Perrine, 19t Dan Burton, 20b
Alan James, 30-31 Doug Perrine, 36-37 Alex Mustard, 37t David
Fleetham, 38-39 Doug Perrine, 46-47 Doug Perrine, 47t Dan Burton, 55b
Michael D. Kern, 71 Rod Williams, 74-75 Alex Mustard , 75t David
Fleetham, 79t Alex Hyde, 85t Alex Hyde, 91b Barry Mansell, 103b Doug
Perrine, 104-105 Jeff Rotman, 107br Inaki Relanzon, 108-109 Jeff
Rotman, 109r Andy Rouse, 112-113 Martin Dohrn; **NHPA** 7t Charles
Hood, 10bl ANT Photo Library, 14-15 T Kitchen & V Hurst, 15t Image
Quest 3D, 19b Daniel Hueclin, 27t Woodfall/Photoshot, 34b, 34-35 Burt
Jones and Maurine Shimlock, 40-41 Dave Pinson, 44-45 ANT Photo
Library, 45b Ken Griffiths, 50-51 Nick Garbutt, 54 E Hanumantha Rao,
56b, 56-57 Charles Hood, 58-59 Larry Ditto, 64b Martin Wendler, 83 Ken
Griffiths, 84-85 Gerard Lacz, 88-89 Ken Griffiths, 89 Photoshot, 90 Mark
Conlin, 95b John Bell, 97b Daniel Heuclin, 98-99 Daniel Heuclin, 99b
Stephen Dalton, 107t Martin Harvey, 108 Jordi Bas Casasj 111 Martin
Harvey, 115t Oceans Image/Photoshot/Saul Gonor; **SPL:** 7b Gerald and
Buff Corsi, Visuals Unlimited, Inc., 18-19 Tom McHugh, 19t Merlin
Tuttle/Bat Conservation International, 22 Sinclair Stammers, 28-29
Matthew Oldfield, 29b WK Fletcher, 31t Visuals Unlimited, 32-33 Solvin
Zankl, 33b Theirry Berrod, Mona Lisa Production, 53b Steve
Gschmeissner, 59 Ken M Highfill, 67b Nature's Images, 68b Simon D
Pollard, 68-69 Barbara Strnadova, 69c James H Robinson, 76br Steve
Gschmeissner, 76-77 Nature's Images, 80b Geoff Kidd, 100t Andy Murch,
Visuals Unlimited, Inc., 111t Andy Murch/Visuals Unlimited, Inc., 111b
Georgette Douwma, 112bl Susumu Nishinaga,115b Andy Murch/Visuals
Unlimited, Inc., 109l John Shaw

Words in **bold** are explained
in the Glossary on page 122.

HOW
SCARY?

Look out for this
rating. It will tell
you how scary each
reptile is.

1—a little scary

2—pretty scary

3—scary

4—QUICK! RUN AWAY!

5—YIKES! TOO LATE!

CONTENTS

Check out
this lemon
shark on
page 34

BASKING SHARK

50 The enormous mouth of a basking shark is large enough to hold a child. Fortunately, a basking shark has no interest in human **prey** because it only eats tiny **plankton**!

DEADLY BITES

Length: Up to 39 ft (1,200 cm)

Habitat: Coasts and deep oceans

Where: Worldwide

Weapons: A VERY large mouth and sieve-like plates

The largest basking sharks weigh up to 21 tons (19 tonnes), five times as much as an elephant.

6

Water and plankton gush into the shark's huge gaping mouth.

The huge slits on the side of a basking shark's head are called gill slits. Fish use **gills** instead of lungs to breathe underwater. Water, which contains oxygen, passes into their mouth and out through the gills. Basking sharks also use their gills to feed. Sieve-like plates in the gills trap any plankton in the water.

Water passes out through the gill slits but the plankton is caught in the gills.

Actual size!

Plankton
Up to 3.2 in (8 cm)

KILLER FACT

Basking sharks often swim near the surface of the sea, and can even leap out of the water!

Mystery Shark

Sharks are mysterious creatures, and scientists need to find out much more about their lifestyles. It is known that basking sharks go on long journeys in spring and summer, but no one knows for sure where they disappear to from November to March.

LONGNOSE SAWSHARK

49 This small shark has a peculiar snout that makes up more than one quarter of its whole body length. The shark uses its strange nose, called a rostrum, as a lethal weapon and to detect prey.

The sides of the long nose are lined with rows of teeth.

Up to 17.6 in (45 cm)

Sawsharks have a small, flat body because they live on the seabed and swim close to the bottom, where they hunt for small fish, squid, and shrimp. Their long nose is called a saw and is lined with long, sharp teeth. Long feelers on the saw, called barbels, are used for touch. They also have teeth in their jaws, which they use for biting.

As they cruise along the seabed, sawsharks use their barbels to detect prey hidden in the sand and mud.

DEADLY BITES

Length: Up to 4.6 ft (140 cm)

Habitat: Seabed in coastal areas

Where: Southern Australia

Weapons: Sensitive detectors and small, needle-sharp teeth

KILLER FACT

Sawsharks sense electricity using organs called ampullae of Lorenzini. These are small, gel-filled holes in their saw.

Electric Sense

These sharks use their saw to swipe at their prey, or to rake through mud and dislodge animals hiding there. Their saw has another great use too—it can detect electricity. All animals use electricity to make their muscles work, and sharks have a super-sense that helps them to detect it.

SCUTIGERA

Creepy-crawlies, spiders, scorpions, and stinging bugs are some of the world's most incredible creatures. They belong to one enormous group of animals, called **invertebrates**.

DEADLY BITES

Length: 4 in. (10 cm)

Habitat: Dark, damp places

Where: Mostly in tropical regions

Weapons: Powerful, venom—injecting claws

HOW SCARY?

Scutigera have well-developed eyes to help them spot their prey.

Scutigera have up to 15 pairs of long legs, which let them run really fast.

Invertebrates are usually small and they don't have bones, but many of them are still fearsome **predators**. This is a giant long-legged centipede called a scutigera. Its body is divided into parts called **segments**, and there is a pair of legs on most segments.

The first pair of legs has claws that can inject a deadly **venom** into a victim. Scutigera feed on other invertebrates, such as beetles.

KILLER FACT

The venom from some scutigera centipedes is strong enough to make a human very sick.

Creepy Legs

Why does any bug need 15 pairs of legs? They aren't just for running—these limbs have another important job to do. This centipede uses its legs to feel its way in the dark, and to find prey.

GILA MONSTER

Gila monsters move slowly, so they pose very little risk to humans.

These lizards are called monsters for a good reason—they have venomous bites. Gila monsters mostly use their venom to defend themselves from other animals.

Gilas are slow-moving desert lizards that prey on birds' eggs and bugs. Like other reptiles, these lizards can use their tongues to sense if food is around. When they flick their tongues, they are "tasting" the air.

Big Digger

The Mexican beaded lizard also has a venomous bite. It uses its large claws to dig burrows, where it hides. It uses its venom to subdue prey, such as birds and small mammals. Its bite is believed to be harmless to humans.

KILLER FACT
Some people keep Gila monsters as pets, which is a bad idea. Eight people have died from Gila bites.

Many venomous animals prefer to warn their enemies away, rather than having to fight them. Gila monsters have black bodies with bold patterns of pink, yellow, or orange. These colors warn predators that the lizards are venomous.

DEADLY BITES

HOW SCARY?

Length: 19.7 in. (50 cm)

Habitat: Deserts

Where: Southwestern United States and Mexico

Weapons: Sharp teeth and a venomous bite

13

ALLIGATOR SNAPPING TURTLE

16 This reptilian predator lurks beneath the murky water in swamps. When it lifts its ugly, scaly head above the water, the bad-tempered animal snaps its jaws and does a great impression of a prehistoric monster. Alligator snapping turtles have one of the nastiest bites of any animal. They grow large and heavy, and live in **freshwater** where they feed on fish. Snapping turtles can reach the age of 100 or more.

With their spiked shells, these reptiles are known as the dinosaurs of the turtle world.

REPTILE BITES

Length: 31.5 in. (80 cm)

Habitat: Lakes, rivers, and swamps

Where: Southeastern USA

Weapons: Scissor-sharp jaws and a vicious bite

HOW SCARY?

Not What It Seems!

When a fish approaches a little red, wriggling worm, it has no idea it is swimming into the jaws of death. For that is no worm, but a lure— a wormlike lump of flesh inside the turtle's mouth that tempts fish and frogs to come close—SNAP!

KILLER FACT

When the turtle sees food, it fills its lure with blood so that it looks red, plump, and very tasty!

SECRETARY BIRD

Raptors have curved bills, which they use to tear the flesh of their prey.

 Birds of prey—raptors—are masters of the sky. Most of them have sharp **talons**, hooked bills, and huge wings that allow them to swoop through the skies looking for prey.

KiLLER FaCt
Secretary birds flap their wings when they attack a snake to draw its attention away from the bird's face.

Secretary birds have long legs that allow them to run at high speed.

Length: 4.9 ft (1.5 m) tall

Habitat: Dry, hot grasslands

Where: Central and southern Africa

Weapons: Large feet and powerful talons

HOW
SCARY?

Secretary birds take to the air during **courtship** as they look for a mate.

Secretary birds are raptors with a difference because they rely on legs, not wings to get around. Although they can fly, these birds spend most of their time on the ground. They walk through long grass searching for grasshoppers, frogs, lizards, tortoises, and even venomous snakes.

When the bird senses another animal, it stamps its feet to flush its prey out of the grass. As the animal tries to escape, the secretary bird chases it, stamping it to death with its large feet.

VAMPIRE BAT

KILLER FACT
Vampire bats have special heat-sensing areas on their noses that help them to find their prey.

44 There are few predators with a worse reputation than the little vampire bat. That's no wonder given their ugly faces, nasty "**fangs**," and a feeding habit of drinking blood.

vampire bats sense warm bodies with their noses.

DEADLY BITES

HOW SCARY?

Length: 3.75 in. (95 mm) long

Habitat: Forests, grasslands, and deserts

Where: Central and South America

Weapons: Sharp little teeth

Vampire bats can run at speeds of up to 5 miles (8 km) per hour.

7 in. (18 cm)

Actual size!

Bats' wings are made of long bones with skin stretched between them.

Bats are mammals. That means they have furry bodies and feed their young with milk. They are the only true flying mammals in the world. Most bats hunt flying prey, such as moths.

Vampire bats, however, feed on blood. They scuttle along the ground searching for warm bodies. A vampire bat bites through its victim's skin with its tiny teeth. As blood oozes out, the bat laps it up.

Pain-Free Feeding

A vampire bat's sharp teeth can tear through skin without the victim feeling pain. The bats produce a chemical that lessens the pain. Grooves in their tongues help blood to pour into their throats.

ELECTRIC EEL

49 Not all predators rely on jaws and claws to catch their prey. Electric eels are fish that **stun** and kill their prey in the most shocking way!

These fish live in the dark, murky waters of the Amazon River, where finding food is a challenge. Electric eels don't have good eyesight. Instead, they use weak electric pulses to find their way, like a **radar** system.

An electric eel also has electric organs along the length of its body. These are used to produce sudden electric shocks that stun the eel's prey or any predators that come too close.

The shock from an electric eel is strong enough to knock a horse off its feet.

Sit and Wait

Moray eels lurk in dark places and wait for food to swim by. They have two sets of jaws to grab their prey and drag it down into their throats. Some morays also have **toxins** on their skins.

Moray eels have large teeth, which they use to tear the flesh of their prey.

21

ARMY ANT

Few things can stop a horde of army ants when they go on a march. By working together, these insects are more powerful than many predators.

KILLER FACT

One **colony** of army ants can kill up to 100,000 bugs in one day. Flies follow them around and eat any leftovers.

Huge jaws can cut and slice, breaking up victims' bodies into small pieces in minutes.

Strength in Numbers

Army ants are social insects that live and work in large groups called colonies. The ants have hooks on their legs, which help them to climb and stick together to make massive nests, called bivouacs, out of their own bodies.

DEADLY BITES

Length: 0.6 in. (15 mm)

Habitat: Hot and humid forests

Where: Australia

Weapons: Powerful jaws, stingers, and lots of friends

HOW SCARY?

The ants build a new nest out of their own bodies in a different place each day.

A few worker ants start the nest, then the whole colony will join in.

23

TASMANIAN DEVIL

KILLER FACT

Tasmanian devils have pink ears, which turn red when they are very angry!

41 Tasmanian devils deserve their name —they are ferocious and extremely bad-tempered. Devils are famous for their blood-curdling nighttime screeches!

Flexible front feet allow devils to hold their food

Food Fight

Tasmanian devils have a great sense of smell. If one devil is feeding, others detect the smell and rush over to share in the feast. Fights sometimes break out over food, but usually the hungry animals just growl at one another.

Tasmanian devils look like small bears, but they are **marsupials** —a type of mammal that gives birth to tiny young that grow inside a pouch.

These predators survive on a diet of meat, which they get by killing animals, such as wallabies and possums, or by scavenging.

Devils can eat nearly half their own body weight in just 30 minutes.

DEADLY BITES

Length: 31.5 in. (80 cm)

Habitat: Bush and scrubland

Where: Tasmania

Weapons: Sharp teeth

HOW SCARY?

SEA SNAKE

40 Sea snakes are venomous snakes that have taken to living and hunting underwater. Some sea snakes give birth to live baby snakes in water, while others come onto land to lay their eggs. They all have to come to the surface to breathe.

DEADLY BITES

Length: 43 in. (110 cm)

Habitat: Shallow ocean water

Where: Pacific and Indian Oceans, Arabian Gulf

Weapons: Fangs with a muscle-eating venom

HOW SCARY?

Sea snakes have more powerful venom than any other snakes, but they rarely bite people and have small fangs. Sea snakes feed on small fish and mollusks.

If they do bite, sea snakes inject only a tiny amount of venom and their victims may not even know they have been bitten at first. The venom causes muscles to break down, and death can occur in a few hours.

Sea snakes swim slowly along the ocean floor looking for prey.

Land and Sea

Sea snakes called kraits come ashore to **shed** their old skins, to mate, and to lay their eggs. The females lay three to 10 eggs in old burrows left by seabirds or under rocks.

Like all snakes, kraits live alone, only coming together to mate.

27

PIRANHA

39 It is said that a group of piranhas can strip the body of a cow to the bones in minutes. The truth is nowhere near as frightening! These fish can live in large groups called shoals, but they mostly feed on bugs, small fish, and shrimps.

Piranha teeth are pointed and razor-sharp.

Actual size!

DEADLY BITES

Length: 13 in. (33 cm) long

Habitat: Rivers

Where: South America

Weapons: Sharp teeth

HOW **SCARY?**

Slice and Slash

Piranhas are able to devour flesh easily, because their strong jaws are lined with large, triangular teeth that interlock perfectly to make a cutting machine that can slash and slice.

Piranhas feed at dawn and dusk, when there is little sunlight and they can hide behind water plants, often in groups of up to 30 fish. Most piranhas attack prey alone.

Occasionally, a number of shoals may gather together into a much larger group to attack and feast on a large animal. However, this is very rare and probably only happens when there is a shortage of food.

29

KILLER BEE

 One bee on its own is unlikely to do much harm to a person. When a group of bees gets together, it's a different matter. A buzzing, angry swarm is terrifying—and dangerous.

Killer bees will chase an animal over longer distances than normal bees.

HOW SCARY?

DEADLY BITES

Length: 0.75 in. (2 cm)

Habitat: Where flowers grow

Where: South and Central America, United States

Weapons: Venomous sting

Fast Fighters

Killer bees are much more likely to attack than ordinary bees. They are quick to create huge angry swarms and can detect people 49 feet (15 m) away from their nests.

Bees die after one sting. Wasps and hornets can keep stinging until they run out of venom.

Bees feed on nectar and pollen from flowers, so they will only sting other animals or people to defend themselves from attack. Most bees have a single sting with tiny hooks called barbs on it. The barbs help the sting to stay in the victim, while venom is pumped into the victim's body, causing pain and swelling.

The sting of a killer bee is no worse than any other bee. It is only a problem when an animal is stung lots of times.

DEADLY SHARKS

A giant fish swims through the ocean, and its body casts a dark shadow on the seabed below. With its huge teeth, super speed, and cold, dead eyes, this shark is one of the world's most impressive predators.

Most sharks are long and thin, but they come in all shapes and sizes. The largest fish in the world is the mighty whale shark. It is harmless to people because it feeds on tiny animals called plankton.

Whale sharks are the giants of the ocean and grow to about 36 feet (11 meters) in length.

Frilled sharks have long, thin bodies and live deep underwater.

KILLER FACT

Sharks have been around for 400 million years, and had few predators—until humans began to hunt them.

All sharks are fish. They eat other animals, such as fish and squid. Sometimes, sharks mistake humans for food and attack them. Most sharks are wary of humans, and try to avoid them. There are some scary ones, however, that are more aggressive.

This blue shark has a pointed nose, or snout, and large eyes so that it can see well in deep water.

LEMON SHARK

37 Lemon sharks are large coastal sharks. They prefer to live in warm, shallow waters near land, especially during the day. At night they swim to deeper water.

Lemon sharks have a wide, flat head.

DEADLY BITES

HOW SCARY?

Length: Up to 11 ft (340 cm)

Habitat: Reefs, mangroves, bays, and river mouths

Where: Warm American waters and West Africa

Weapons: Special electrical sensors and triangular teeth

Lemon sharks have small eyes and poor eyesight. The coastal waters where they live are often cloudy, so eyesight is not a great help in finding prey. Instead, these fish have special magnetic **sensors** in their snout, which help them to find fish and shelled animals on the seabed.

Sharksuckers

Remoras, or sharksuckers, are long, thin fish with a special ability. They have a sucker on the top of their head, which they use to stick to a shark or other large fish and hitch a ride. They feed off any scraps that the shark does not eat.

Lemon sharks get their name from the yellow-brown color of their skin.

EGGS AND PUPS

Most fish lay eggs that **hatch** into baby fish. Sharks are special, though. Many of them don't lay eggs, they give birth to their young instead. Young sharks are called **pups**.

Lemon sharks can give birth to as many as 17 pups in a single year.

Most mother sharks keep their pups inside their body while they grow. This means the pups are protected from predators for as long as possible. When the pups are born they are able to swim away. Sharks don't look after their pups.

Mermaid's Purse

Sharks that do lay eggs, such as catsharks, lay the eggs in a thick, rubbery case called a mermaid's purse. These egg cases often have curly strings, which attach them to rocks or seaweed to stop them from floating away. The shark pups grow inside for up to ten months.

Up to 3.2 in (8 cm)

Actual size!

This newborn lemon shark pup swims away from its mother.

KILLER FACT

Pups growing inside their mother may eat each other before they are even born. Sometimes only one or two pups survive.

JUMPER ANT

36 There are at least 10,000 **species** of ant in the world. Most ants can bite or sting—or make venomous droplets that inflict pain. Their venom is similar to that of bees.

This jumper ant has managed to catch a bee in its jaws.

Bulldog and jumper ants are larger than most ants, and use their excellent eyesight to find other ants and bees to prey on. They are aggressive insects that will leap into action when they are threatened— and can actually jump at a victim!

Big Stingers

Little black bullet ants are said to inflict the most painful of all ant stings. Fire ants use their stings to defend the large homes they make and share. They use their pincers to grab hold of their victim and just keep on stinging!

As jumper ants sink their large jaws into an animal or human, they use a stinger to inject powerful chemicals that cause great pain.

DEADLY BITES

Length: 1 in. (25 mm)

Habitat: Forests

Where: Australia

Weapons: Strong jaws and a painful stinger

HOW SCARY?

LONOMIA

KILLER FACT

Scientists hope to be able to make life-saving medicine using lonomia venom.

35 A killer caterpillar's deadly spines send out a clear warning to predators— this creature will not make a tasty snack.

The colorful caterpillar becomes a brown moth.

A lonomia caterpillar will become a moth one day. While it is still young, however, a caterpillar's job is to eat and grow—and avoid being eaten itself.

Most caterpillars rely on **camouflage** to stay safe. They are often green or brown so they can hide on the plants they eat. Lonomia caterpillars, however, are covered with sharp spines that they want predators to notice!

Prickles and Poison

The sharp spines warn predators, such as birds, lizards, and frogs, that this soft-bodied mini monster is carrying a nasty venom. The spines break when they pierce a victim's skin, and the venom enters its body.

The bright colors help to warn predators.

If enough venom gets into a person's body, it can cause severe pain, bruising, and even death!

DEADLY BITES

Length: 2.4 in. (6 cm) long

Habitat: Rain forests

Where: South America

Weapons: Venom-tipped spines all over its body

HOW SCARY?

PARALYSIS TICK

KILLER FACT

Other ticks also cause disease. They carry bacteria that infect the wounds they make.

34 Ticks are insects with eight legs, like spiders, and a blood-sucking lifestyle. Most ticks cause little harm, but some of them carry a deadly secret.

These bugs are **parasites**, which means they feed on another animal while it is still alive. Ticks have sharp mouthparts that pierce a hole in a victim's flesh, and inject a liquid to stop blood from **clotting**. The ticks suck blood until their bodies are large and swollen, and then they fall to the ground.

Actual size!

Before feeding

After feeding

Australian paralysis ticks have another nasty trick. They don't just suck blood—they inject a venom that causes the victim to become **paralyzed**. Without treatment, the victim may die.

Paralysis ticks prey on many kinds of animal, including pets and people.

HOW SCARY?

Tick **larvae** have three pairs of legs, while adult ticks have four pairs.

Only a small number of tick eggs will actually hatch.

Monster Moms

Female ticks must feed on blood before they can lay eggs, and this is when they inject dangerous toxins. They lay up to 3,000 eggs at a time. Lazy males sometimes suck blood from the females!

43

GRAY REEF SHARK

33 Sometimes divers and snorkelers come face-to-face with one of the world's most threatening sharks—the gray reef shark. These hunters patrol coral reefs in groups.

Most sharks are **solitary** animals and live alone. Gray reef sharks, however, often swim in groups in quiet spots during the day. At night they go their separate ways to hunt. When a gray reef shark is feeling threatened it raises its snout, arches its back, and swims with a swaying motion. This menacing behavior warns enemies to move away—or prepare to be attacked.

44

Fishy Feasts

Gray reef sharks feed on squid, octopus, and small shelled animals such as shrimp and lobsters. They also prey on the colorful fish that live among the reefs, such as these beautiful butterfly fish.

DEADLY BITES

HOW SCARY?

Length: Up to 8.5 ft (260 cm)

Habitat: Coral reefs

Where: Indian and Pacific Oceans

Weapons: Lots of friends, great agility, and 13–14 rows of teeth

CHIMPANZEE

32 Some animal experts think chimpanzees are among the most impressive of all predators. They are fast and clever, and work in a gang to track and kill other animals.

When they feel threatened, chimps bare their teeth.

Toolmakers

Like humans, chimps make tools to use in a hunt. They strip bark from a branch, sharpen it, and use it to kill small animals. They also use twigs to dig into termite nests.

KILLER FACT
Chimpanzees are our closest living relatives and some of the cleverest animals alive.

For a long time, scientists thought chimps enjoyed a diet of fruits, leaves, nuts, roots, and bugs. Then it was discovered they also prey on pigs and monkeys, and even kill chimps from other families.

These apes hunt cooperatively, which means they work together and have different jobs to do. One chimp might chase a monkey through the trees, while another blocks its escape route and a third waits to **ambush** it.

HOW SCARY?

DEADLY BITES

Length: 35.4 in. (90 cm) tall

Habitat: Tropical rain forest

Where: Central Africa

Weapons: Hands and teeth

HONEY BADGER

31 Honey badgers may have a sweet-sounding name, but they are totally fearless predators. These beasts are programmed to strike and kill, and they are not fussy about what they attack.

KILLER FACT
Honey badgers can kill small crocodiles and pythons that are more than 10 feet (3 m) long!

Badgers live alone and only come together once a year to breed.

These predators explore every avenue in pursuit of food. They dig holes in the ground, searching for worms and bugs, climb trees to raid honey and grubs from bees' nests, and even scamper to upper branches to steal eggs from raptor nests!

It takes courage to face a lion devouring its prey head on, and then scare that lion away. But that's what honey badgers are willing to do when they have their sights set on lunch.

Thick skin around the neck and small ears protect the honey badger from injury in fights.

Best Friends

Honeyguide birds perch near to bees' nests, and show honey badgers where to dig or climb. Once the badger has opened a nest, the bird swoops in to feast on bees and beeswax.

KOMODO DRAGON

DEADLY BITES

Length: 9.8 ft. (3 m)

Habitat: Scrubland and grassland

Where: Komodo Island, Indonesia

Weapons: Big claws and a venomous bite

HOW SCARY?

30 Few predators are more fascinating than the Komodo dragon. These huge reptiles rule the island of Komodo in Indonesia, but there are fewer than 5,000 of them left in the wild.

Komodos were not discovered until about 100 years ago.

Komodos are the world's heaviest lizards, and a male can weigh more than an adult human. They have strength rather than speed, and lie in wait for passing prey to ambush it. Komodos aren't fussy and will eat almost anything they find, including deer, pigs— and even humans!

Deadly Bite

When a Komodo spots its prey, it springs to action and uses its sharp claws to hold the animal down. A quick bite with its sharp teeth allows the Komodo to pass venom into the prey's body. The injured animal runs away, but will soon weaken from its wound. The Komodo can then stroll over and finish its meal.

One side of a Komodo's teeth has jagged **serrations**.

KING COBRA

A king cobra puffs out its hood when threatened to make itself look bigger.

29 The king cobra is the longest of all venomous snakes, and can reach a length of more than 16 feet (5 m). It's so big, a king cobra can raise enough of its body off the ground to look a human in the eye!

As hunters, king cobras have powerful venom and size on their side, but they prey on other snakes, not people. When they are scared, these snakes rear up, spread out their hoods, and hiss. Putting on this scary show is a type of defense and it should make most enemies think twice before coming any closer.

DEADLY BITES

Length: 16 ft. (5 m)

Habitat: Forests, grassland, and scrubland

Where: Southeast Asia

Weapons: Fangs with deadly venom

KILLER FACT

King cobras rarely kill people, but Indian cobras attack at least 10,000 people every year in India alone.

Mamba!

28 Everyone in Africa knows to look out for this snake, which is one of the world's most dangerous predators. Mambas can slither faster than a person can run, are active during daytime, and have a deadly bite. Thankfully, mambas normally hunt birds and small animals—not people.

One bite from a mamba can kill an adult human in minutes.

Actual size!

HAMMERHEAD SHARK

27 There are about 400 different types, or species, of shark and some of the strangest-looking ones are called hammerheads. Like its relatives—such as the mallethead sharks—the great hammerhead has an extraordinary appearance.

A hammerhead's nostrils are far apart, helping it to sense the direction of different smells.

A hammerhead's head is huge and wide, with eyes positioned right at the very ends. This shape probably helps the predator to move through water and change direction. The position of its eyes helps the shark to focus on its prey more easily, and work out how far away it is.

KILLER FACT

Hammerheads like to feast on venomous stingrays, and can even eat the venom-filled tails!

Fight for Life

Hammerheads can live for about 30 years, but few of them reach that great age. They are endangered, which means that they are at risk of becoming **extinct** because too many have been fished from the sea. They are also **cannibals**, and adults often prey on young hammerheads.

HOW SCARY?

SHARK BITES

Length: Up to 20 ft (610 cm)

Habitat: Coastal waters and offshore

Where: Worldwide

Weapons: Good **binocular** vision and sharp teeth

55

CORAL SNAKE

Coral snakes hunt lizards, snakes, frogs, nesting birds, and small mammals.

26 Look at the two snakes shown on these pages. Can you tell the difference? The coral snake in the main picture has red and yellow bands that warn predators of its venomous bite, but the milk snake opposite is a harmless copycat.

HOW SCARY?

REPTILE BITES

Length: 35 in. (90 cm)

Habitat: Forests

Where: The Americas

Weapons: Fangs with deadly venom

The yellow bands on this snake's body are next to the red color. This means it is a deadly coral snake.

There are about 40 different types of coral snake, with different patterns of colored bands. Most live in burrows and only come out at night, so humans rarely encounter these venomous creatures.

Coral snakes need to keep jabbing at a victim to inject all their venom, so although the venom is deadly in large amounts, it is rare for people to die following an attack.

Smart Mimic

Milk snakes can bite, but they don't have venom. Their cunning disguise, however, makes them look like venomous coral snakes so predators stay away. A rhyme helps identify some of these colorful snakes: *If red touches yellow, it can kill a fellow, if red touches black, it's a friend of Jack.*

57

TIGER

25 Tigers are the largest of all the big cats, and one of the largest of all predators. These majestic animals combine beauty, **stealth**, and speed with a deadly instinct to kill.

A tiger's stripes camouflage it, keeping it hidden from its prey.

Most tigers live and hunt alone. They patrol their areas, which are called territories, looking for clues that other tigers or other animals are nearby. Tigers have a great sense of smell, which helps them to find prey hiding in the jungle.

DEADLY BITES

Length: Up to 9.1 ft. (280 cm)

Habitat: Forests, mountains, and jungles

Where: Southeast Asia

Weapons: Teeth and claws

The Siberian tiger lives high in the mountains, where it hunts deer and small mammals.

Big Appetites

Tigers can attack large animals, such as pigs, deer, and monkeys. They may even hunt baby elephants and rhinoceroses. Once it has killed its prey, a tiger will **gorge** itself on meat, eating up to 88 pounds (40 kg) at one time. It may keep returning to the carcass to feed on it over the next few days.

KILLER FACT

There used to be eight species of tiger, but three of them have become extinct in the last 60 years.

ANACONDA

24 Some fearsome reptiles take life at a slow pace, only stirring into action when hunger strikes. The **constrictor** snakes may survive for several months on one big meal!

Pythons and boas don't use deadly venom to kill their prey—they squeeze them to death instead. Anacondas are a type of boa. They spend most of their lives in water, but slither onto land to hunt. They ambush animals that come to the water to drink, grabbing them in their coils.

Anacondas wrap themselves around their prey and squeeze until it **suffocates**.

KiLLER FACT
Anacondas don't lay eggs. They give birth to up to 80 young snakes at a time.

A large anaconda is heavier than an adult human.

Massive Monsters

Anacondas are big enough to prey on large animals, including caimans, deer, and even people. A record-breaking anaconda measured 27.7 feet (8.4 m) long—as long as the net on a tennis court—and 43 inches (110 cm) around its middle.

REPTILE BITES

Length: 28 ft. (8.5 m)

Habitat: Rain forests, grasslands, and rivers

Where: South America

Weapons: Constricting coils

HOW SCARY?

BLACK CAIMAN

When caiman are underwater, special flaps close over their nostrils and ears to stop water from getting in.

23 Caimans are members of the crocodile and alligator family. Although they are great predators themselves, some types of caiman are close to extinction because humans hunt them for their skins.

KILLER FACT
Caimans attack people for three main reasons: to eat, to defend their homes, or to defend their young.

Caimans use their excellent eyesight and sense of smell to hunt fish, waterbirds, and turtles. They spend most of the day floating in water, but when they come ashore at night, they may hunt mammals, especially **capybaras**, dogs, pigs, and deer. They have been known to attack people.

HOW SCARY?

REPTILE BITES

Length: 19.7 ft. (6 m)

Habitat: Rivers and lakes

Where: South America

Weapons: Sharp teeth

The black caiman is the largest predator in the Amazon rain forest

Actual size!

Head is 2–3 in. (6–8 cm) long

Caring Mother

Female black caimans lay up to 60 eggs in a nest near slow-flowing water. They stay on their nest to protect their eggs from predators, and take care of the babies after they hatch.

BIRD-EATING SPIDER

22 This is no mini monster—it's a maxi monster! The goliath bird-eating spider is the heaviest spider in the world, and it attacks birds, lizards, and frogs.

All spiders have eight legs and a body that is divided into two parts. They can sense other animals through their legs, which are very sensitive to movement.

Goliath bird-eating spiders make a hissing noise to warn predators away. If that doesn't work, they rear up on their back legs and expose their fangs, ready to bite. They can also shoot irritating hairs at attackers.

Spiders use the hairs on their legs to sense the movements of other animals that are nearby.

Actual size!

BUG BITES

Length: 10.25 in. (26 cm) across

Habitat: Mountain rain forests

Where: South America

Weapons: Enormous fangs, venom, and irritating hairs

A Nasty Bite

The body of a goliath bird-eating spider can measure more than 4 inches (10 cm) and each fang is about 0.75 inches (2 cm) long. These spiders can inject venom when they bite.

KiLLER FACT

Females can live for 20 years. Males rarely live for more than six years because they die after **mating**.

ASSASSIN BUG

21 Assassin bugs may be small, but they are deadly predators. These blood-sucking beasts hunt prey using a variety of cunning tricks.

Assassin bugs hold on to prey using sticky pads on their front legs. Needle-like mouthparts pierce the victim's body and inject a toxic liquid that turns flesh into a tasty juice. A big cockroach takes just three seconds to die—and the bug then sucks up its liquid meal.

Some assassin bugs ambush their prey, or trick them by dangling dead insects near the entrance to their homes. Others pretend to be flies caught in a web, so they can pounce on the spider that comes to investigate.

The toxic **saliva** in the bite can cause blindness.

This assassin bug is attacking a termite worker.

66

An assassin bug's bite is one of the most painful insect bites in the world.

Kissing Bug

Kissing bugs are assassin bugs that prey on larger animals, such as mammals, birds, and people. They suck blood from their victims and pass on the deadly Chagas disease.

BUG BITES

Length: 1.6 in. (4 cm)

Habitat: Many, from yards to forests

Where: Worldwide

Weapons: Needle-sharp bite that can inject bacteria

HOW SCARY?

WOLVERINE

20 These weasel-like animals are no bigger than a dog, but they are brave and fierce enough to attack a bear.

Wolverines live in the world's cold north, where food is scarce. They have long, thick fur to keep them warm.

These fearless predators are always on the move, and chase animals much bigger than themselves, such as deer. They leap boldly at their prey, grabbing them in their strong jaws.

Wolverines can kill prey that are many times bigger than them.

A wolverine's jaws are as powerful as those of a crocodile. They can crunch through the large bones of caribou and deer.

KILLER FACT

Wolverines are not just predators. They also scavenge, which means they eat dead animals they find.

Broad, furry paws help wolverines walk on icy surfaces.

PREDATOR BITES

Length: 39.4 in. (100 cm)

Habitat: Forests and mountains

Where: Northerly regions

Weapons: Massive jaws and crunching teeth

HOW SCARY?

WOLF

19 Wolves often appear in fairy tales and legends as wily killers. They are certainly smart predators with a nose for danger.

During the winter, wolves grow thick, fluffy fur.

PREDATOR BITES

Length: 4.9 ft. (150 cm)

Habitat: Cool forests and mountains

Where: Northerly places

Weapons: Sharp teeth and powerful jaws

The alpha female is the only female in the pack that gives birth to cubs.

Rare Beasts

Wolves once roamed large parts of the world, but they are now mostly found in northern forests. They live in groups called packs that are ruled by a top male and female called the **alpha pair.**

70

When prey is nearby, wolves give chase and can run for hours. They work as a team, and may split up to confuse their prey and attack from all sides.

Powerful jaws can crush bones.

KILLER FACT
Gray wolves are the largest members of the dog family, and all of our pet dogs are descended from wolves.

Wolves keep in contact with each other over long distances by howling.

Like all dogs, wolves have an incredible sense of smell, and can detect prey, such as rabbits, by their smell more than a mile away. They can also hear sounds that are 6 miles (10 km) away.

BLACK WIDOW SPIDER

18 Black widow spiders are known as dangerous, but it's insects that have most to fear from their venomous attacks. Black widows set traps and deliver lethal bites.

KILLER FACT
Occasionally, female black widows kill and eat males after mating with them.

The spiders add drops of glue to the threads of a web to make them more sticky.

Black widows build messy webs using special bristles on their legs. Once the victim is trapped in the web, a spider can inject it with venom that is up to 15 times stronger than that of a rattlesnake, but in much smaller amounts.

Smart Moves

Most male spiders have to impress the females before mating. A male Australian redback spends more than an hour dancing for a female, but if she doesn't like his dance, she might eat him!

Black widows only bite people to defend themselves and their bites are rarely fatal

BUG BITES

Length: 0.6 in. (15 mm)

Habitat: Warm, dark places

Where: North America

Weapons: A nasty bite, a sticky web, and strong venom

HOW SCARY?

SKELETONS AND SCALES

Most fish are bony fish. They have a bony skeleton that gives their body shape, power, and strength. Sharks, however, don't have bones. Instead, their skeleton is made from a strong, bendy material called **cartilage**.

KILLER FACT

It isn't just shark teeth that can hurt—their skin can too. Its rough surface can tear the skin from a swimmer's leg.

Shark denticles

This swell shark has a spotted pattern to help it hide against the seabed.

Shark skin is covered with scales that are coated with enamel—the same tough material that makes our teeth hard. These scales are called **denticles**. Denticles help water to move smoothly over a shark, so it can swim fast.

Colors and Patterns

Some sharks have interesting patterns. Colors and patterns can help a shark to stay hidden from view. This is called camouflage. This wobbegong shark's strange shape and frilled mouth make a good disguise.

TIGER SHARK

17 Meet the terrifying tiger shark—one of the most dangerous sharks in the world. These predators have been compared to garbage cans because they will try to eat almost anything.

They are called tiger sharks because their skin is marked with dark stripes and spots.

Tiger sharks are hungry, fearless hunters that come close to the shore in search of food. They spend most of the day slowly cruising through the water, but can suddenly burst into speed when they spy something tasty. They hunt sea turtles, clams, stingrays, sea snakes, seals, birds, and squid.

KILLER FACT

Tiger shark teeth are serrated, like a saw. As the sharks bite, they pull their head from side to side and saw the flesh.

SHARK BITES

Length: Up to 18 ft (550 cm)

Habitat: Coasts, reefs, harbors, and river mouths

Where: Warm tropical waters

Weapons: Replaceable teeth

Scavengers

These sharks are **scavengers**, which means they are not fussy eaters and will feast on dead meat. They have been found with bottles, lumps of wood, potatoes, car tires—and even drums—in their stomach!

77

FUNNEL-WEB SPIDER

 Funnel-web spiders have glossy, brown, or black bodies, and do not look all that scary. But looks can be deceiving ...

A funnel-web spider waits in its tunnel for a tasty treat to pass by.

DEADLY BITES

Length: 1.2 in. (3 cm)

Habitat: Homes, yards, and forests

Where: Southeast Australia

Weapons: Enormous fangs

HOW SCARY?

Hidden from View

Funnel-web spiders hide in dark, damp places. They live in burrows and weave silken trip lines around the entrances. When a little creature walks on the silk thread, the spider feels the vibrations and leaps out of its burrow to attack.

The venom affects the **nervous systems** of humans and monkeys, but not other mammals.

KILLER FACT

Funnel-web spiders can't swim, but they can stay alive in water for up to 30 hours.

Of all funnel-web spiders, the most dangerous are male Sydney funnel-web spiders, which have such deadly venom they can kill their prey in seconds. They have fangs nearly 0.4 in. (1 cm) long.

When it is time to mate, male Sydney funnel-web spiders come out of their burrows to look for females. They search relentlessly, and attack anyone who gets in their way.

KILLER WHALE

15 There is one predator that even a great white shark fears—the killer whale, or orca. These marine mammals are easy to spot, with their striking black and white markings.

Teamwork

Killer whales often live and travel in groups called pods. They work as a team to catch their prey. Some pods just eat fish, while others prefer to hunt seals or other whales.

Killer whales are very daring in their hunting. Some even risk **beaching** themselves to snatch seals from the shoreline.

A killer whale tries to grab a sea lion from the beach. The whale must be very careful not to get stuck.

Killer whales are successful hunters because they have a range of hunting strategies and prey on many types of animal. Dolphins, whales, sharks, turtles, seals, and fish all have good reason to be afraid of killer whales!

HOW
SCARY?

DEADLY BITES

Length: 29.5 ft. (9 m)

Habitat: Ocean

Where: Worldwide

Weapons: Tail, head, and teeth

BROWN RECLUSE SPIDER

 Brown recluse spiders may be small, but they are fanged, fast-moving, eight-legged predators.

The pedipalps are short limbs on either side of the head.

Brown recluse spiders use special legs, called pedipalps, to grab and hold their prey while they inject venom with fangs. The bite of a brown recluse is usually painless to a human, but within a few hours a sore wound develops, which needs to be treated by a doctor.

This spider's venom works by eating away at the skin, and can cause death in some people.

Most spiders have eight eyes, but brown recluse spiders have six. They build large, sticky webs that look like silken sheets, and often make their homes in dark corners of houses. They use their webs to hold their egg sacs, not to catch prey, which they hunt at night.

DEADLY BITES

Length: 0.6 in. (15 mm)

Habitat: Mostly tropical areas

Where: Worldwide

Weapons: Sharp fangs and a skin–eating venom

HOW SCARY?

TAIPAN

13 Snakes are smooth-scaled, slithering predators. These reptiles have speed and super senses, and some can inject a deadly venom using their fearsome fangs.

KILLER FACT

A taipan has enough venom to kill 250,000 mice, 150,000 rats— or 100 people!

The taipan is also called the "fierce snake."

The deadly taipan lives in Australian deserts and is the most venomous snake in the world. Taipans belong to a group of snakes that are called elapids.

Like most snakes, taipans hunt small animals to eat, even entering their burrows. They only attack people if they are feeling scared.

A Quick Death

Most elapids are fast-moving snakes that can strike with lightning speed. When elapid snakes bite their prey, venom runs down grooves on a fang's surface or through a canal in the center of each fang. The venom usually affects the victim's nervous system, so it cannot move or breathe.

Taipans have needlelike fangs at the fronts of their mouths.

DEADLY BITES

Length: 12 ft. (3.7 m)

Habitat: Forests, deserts, and grassland

Where: Northern Australia

Weapons: Needle-sharp fangs with deadly venom

HOW SCARY?

85

ALLIGATOR

12 American alligators were so heavily hunted by humans for their skins, that they were in danger of dying out completely. Today, these impressive predators are protected.

This alligator is hiding under the algae, waiting for unsuspecting prey to pass by.

KILLER FACT
Although they breathe air, alligators can stay underwater for up to six hours at a time.

Like other reptiles, alligators need to keep warm to move at speed, so they spend most of the day floating in water and **basking** in the sun. When they float, alligators can stay almost completely motionless. Just their eyes and the tips of their noses poke above the water—looking for prey and smelling the air.

DEADLY BITES

Length: 16.4 ft (5 m)

Habitat: Coasts, mangrove swamps, rivers, and lakes

Where: United States

Weapons: 74–80 teeth

Smaller young alligators often gather together in large groups.

Baby alligators are just 8.7 in. (22 cm) long when they hatch.

Taking Care

Female alligators build huge nests and lay about 45 eggs at a time. After the baby alligators hatch, their mother carefully lifts them in her mouth and takes each one down to the water.

SCORPION

The huge imperial scorpion has powerful pincers to kill its prey. Smaller, weaker scorpions rely on venomous stings to defeat their victims.

DEADLY BITES

Length: 8 in. (20 cm)

Habitat: Hot, dark, and dry places

Where: Worldwide

Weapons: Powerful claws and a venom-filled stinger

HOW SCARY?

The imperial scorpion holds the record as the world's largest scorpion.

Female scorpions give birth to live young and carry the babies on their backs.

An emperor scorpion can grow to 8 inches (20 cm) long. Its claws are covered with hairs that help this predator sense the movement of small animals nearby. It has strong pincers to grab and crush its prey, and only uses its venomous sting to attack large animals or to defend itself.

Death Stalker

Death stalker scorpions have large pincers, but these are too weak to hold their prey, such as insects, for long. When a scorpion has been successful in a hunt, it must quickly deliver a deadly blow. It bends its long tail over its head, and plunges the sharp, curved sting into its victim.

KILLER FACT

Death stalker scorpions are very aggressive, and can deliver lethal venom to humans.

RATTLESNAKE

8 If you hear the distinctive noise of a rattlesnake shaking its tail, you know it's time to escape—fast! These are supreme hunting serpents with speed, strength, and some unbelievable superskills.

Actual size

The snake's rattle is at the end of its tail

Rattlesnakes spend most of the day sunbathing, or hiding under rocks and in burrows. They hunt at dusk, when small mammals come out to find food, and can strike with amazing speed.

HOW SCARY?

When a snake flicks its tongue, it is smelling and tasting the air. When the snake pulls its tongue back into its mouth, it senses the smell using a special organ in the roof of its mouth.

KILLER FACT

The Western diamondback is the most dangerous of all rattlesnakes, and its bites can prove deadly to humans.

Seeing in the Dark

Rattlesnakes can hunt in total darkness. They use special heat-detecting pits to find small animals. This super sense helps the snake to build up a picture of where an animal is, its size, shape, and even its movements.

Heat-detecting pit

91

PUFF ADDER

The body is thick, with a **girth** of up to 16 in. (40 cm).

When a puff adder is feeling scared, it puffs out its body to make itself look larger and hisses. But this snake has little to fear from anyone—it is one of Africa's deadliest snakes.

KILLER FACT

Puff adders are responsible for nearly two-thirds of all snakebites in Africa.

Puff adders are the most common snakes in Africa, and often live close to humans. They kill more people in Africa than any other kind of snake.

The pattern on its skin keeps the snake well hidden.

DEADLY BITES

Length: 39 in. (100 cm)

Habitat: Grassland and scrubland

Where: Central and southern Africa

Weapons: Ambushing skills, enormous fangs, and deadly venom

HOW **SCARY?**

Hiding

With brown and cream camouflage, puff adders can hide in the undergrowth, waiting to ambush small animals. Their large, heavy bodies slither silently between plants, but when prey is close, these cumbersome snakes turn into speedy hunters. If they encounter a human, puff adders can easily deliver enough venom to kill.

A puff adder's long fangs can pierce leather!

93

ON THE MOVE

A pointed nose and a streamlined body help a shark to swim fast.

Moving through water is harder work than moving through air. Most fish have a **streamlined** body shape, which means their body moves through water easily. So fast swimmers usually have a long, slender shape.

Most sharks move quickly through water, and their body is packed with powerful muscles. The world's fastest shark is the shortfin mako. It is thought that this shark may reach speeds of 53 miles (88 kilometers) per hour—that's about the same speed as a cheetah chasing its prey.

Pectoral fins control direction and movements up and down.

The dorsal fin helps the fish to swim in S-shaped curves and stops it from rolling over.

The caudal, or tail, fin helps propel the shark through water.

KILLER FACT

Sharks have a big, oily liver that helps them to float, but if they stop swimming they sink to the seabed.

Slow Movers

Some sharks prefer life in the slow lane. They live on the seabed and move by swimming and almost "walking" with their fins. This leopard catshark roams the sandy seabed at night, searching for shellfish and small fish.

BULL SHARK

6 This broad, strong shark is known for its aggressive nature. Bull sharks are described as "short tempered," which means they are always ready for a fight!

Bull sharks usually live and hunt on their own.

Almost all sharks live in seas and oceans, where the water is salty. Bull sharks are more adaptable. They live in shallow coastal waters, but they also swim up rivers, and have even been found in freshwater lakes. Spotting a bull shark can be difficult, because they often swim in cloudy water.

Some experts believe that the bull shark is the deadliest shark in the world.

DEADLY BITES

Length: Up to 11 ft (340 cm)

Habitat: Coasts, rivers, and bays

Where: Warm tropical waters

Weapons: Very aggressive, rapid acceleration, razor-sharp teeth

Lateral line

Sensitive Senses

Bull sharks have poor eyesight. Instead, they rely on a superb sense of smell. Like other sharks, they have a sensitive line that runs along their body, called the lateral line. This detects movement and vibrations in the water.

SHARKS AND PEOPLE

Humans are much more deadly than sharks. It is rare for sharks to attack people, and most of those human victims do survive an attack. People, however, kill up to 120 million sharks every year.

Many of these majestic marine predators are now in grave danger of becoming extinct. That means they will disappear from our planet forever. Sharks are fished from the seas for their meat and their fins, which are used in soup. They are also caught accidentally by fishermen who are hoping to catch other fish to eat.

This dogfish died after getting tangled in a fisherman's net.

Shark cages allow scientists to study sharks close-up, without either the divers or the sharks getting into trouble.

Saving Sharks

We need sharks in our seas. They are part of the ocean ecosystem, and they play an important part in keeping the oceans healthy and in balance. We can help by not buying shark products, and by learning as much as we can about these beautiful fish.

KILLER FACT

There used to be ten times as many sharks in the oceans as there are today.

99

LION

5 Lions are unusual big cats. Like most predators, they have deadly weapons to catch and kill their prey. Unlike most predators, lions hunt in groups.

Even friendly, **tame** lions can suddenly turn on a human and decide it's time to eat!

Lions are strong and smart. They have superb senses of sight and smell, which help them to find antelope and zebras. They live and hunt in family groups called prides.

KILLER FACT
Lion hunts are most successful on moonless nights. In the dark, prey can't see the lions stalking them.

Lionesses do most of the hunting. They stalk their prey, creeping up close until it is time for the kill. They share the meat with the pride. An adult male can eat up to 95 lb. (43 kg) at one time—the weight of a 13-year-old child!

Canine tooth

Actual size!

2 in. (5 cm)

Reasons to Kill

Hunting for food is hard work, but it's worth the effort. Meat is packed with energy, so a predator only needs to eat occasionally. In contrast, animals that eat plants need to spend most of their time feeding to get enough energy to live.

POLAR BEAR

 Brown bears and polar bears are the world's largest land meat-eaters. Brown bears have a fearsome reputation, but they do not match polar bears' ruthless approach to hunting.

Polar bears eat most in the winter months, when they can hunt on the sea ice.

PREDATOR BITES

Length: 11.1 ft. (3.4 m)

Habitat: The ocean and icy regions

Where: Arctic and Northern Canada

Weapons: Sharp teeth and claws

HOW SCARY?

Polar bears are ferocious hunters and they rely almost entirely on a diet of meat from whales, dolphins, and seals. There are few plants in the Arctic so, unlike other bears, they cannot feed on berries or fruits.

Polar bears can survive for up to eight months without food. They are great swimmers, and can run as fast as a human for short stretches. A bear may walk as far as 3,100 miles (5,000 km) in just one year.

12 in. (30 cm)

Seal Meal

To catch their favorite meal of seal, polar bears must wait by an ice hole, where seals pop up to breathe. A quick swipe with its massive claws and a snap of the jaws is all it takes to catch lunch.

Huge feet help bears walk on snow and swim quickly.

SALTWATER CROCODILE

When the world's largest reptile decides it is hungry, no one is safe. The saltwater crocodile, or "saltie," is a fearsome hunter that uses stealth, speed, and strength to kill.

DEADLY BITES

Length: 8.2–23 ft. (2.5–7 m)

Habitat: Coasts, mangrove swamps, rivers, and lakes

Where: Southeast Asia to Australia

Weapons: 64–68 teeth

HOW SCARY?

Saltwater crocodiles live in warm waters in Asia and the Pacific Ocean. These massive crocodilians can grow to at least 16 feet (5 m) long, but it is thought that some males may grow to more than 23 feet (7 m) from snout to tail-tip. Despite their huge and heavy bodies, crocodiles can move with great speed on land and can outrun a human.

Salties hunt fish, mammals, and birds. They clamp their jaws around their prey and, gripping tightly, sink below the water. Then the crocodiles begin the "death roll," and spin their bodies until the prey is drowned.

Salties have 64–68 pointed teeth in their long jaws.

3.3 in. (8.5 cm)

Death Roll

Crocodiles can bite, but they can't chew. Their piercing teeth are perfect for grabbing hold of prey, but they might not kill it. That's why crocodiles perform a death roll.

KILLER FACT
Crocodiles sometimes hunt in groups, which suggests they are smarter than most reptiles.

MOSQUITO

2 At their best, mosquitoes are buzzing, biting bloodsuckers. At their worst, these flies are among the world's most dangerous pests.

Male mosquitoes mostly feed from flowers, but females have to feed on blood before they can lay their eggs. They search out mammals and birds to attack, and have long mouthparts that pierce skin.

The tip of the mouthpart is needle-sharp.

As they break the skin, mosquitoes inject saliva to stop blood from clotting so they can keep sucking it up. Mosquitoes are parasites, and the animals they feed upon are called **hosts**.

HOW
SCARY?

Mosquito's abdomen swells with blood.

Females find prey by detecting carbon dioxide (the gas we breathe out) and body warmth

KiLLER FACT

About 250 million people are infected with malaria every year, causing nearly one million of them to die.

Deadly Disease

Some mosquitoes, especially those that live in hot countries, carry bacteria that cause sickness. When the flies move from host to host, they pass on the bacteria, which can lead to deadly diseases such as malaria and dengue fever.

GREAT WHITE SHARK

A great white's bite is three times more powerful than a lion's bite.

Does the great white shark really deserve to be called the oceans' most vicious predator? It is certainly well equipped to hunt, catch, and kill its prey.

DEADLY BITES

Length: Up to 22 ft (680 cm)

Habitat: Cool coastal waters and deep oceans

Where: Worldwide

Weapons: Powerful muscles, amazing speed, and a crunching bite

Great whites are special sharks. They are big and powerful, they swim at speed and over great distances, and they are extremely skilled hunters. They can detect a single drop of blood in nearby water.

Great whites usually swim alone, but are sometimes seen hunting in pairs or small groups.

Great whites have 50 to 60 large teeth that are arranged in rows. When one tooth falls out it is quickly replaced.

Bite and Shake

When a great white takes a bite of its prey, it shakes its head from side to side. As it does so, the large triangular teeth saw through prey, chomping off large pieces of meat.

109

TOP 20
DEADLY FACTS

Sharks can see in dark water,
but they are probably color-blind.

Spitting cobras blind their victims
by spraying venom.

Some prehistoric scorpions grew to
lengths of 31.5 in. (80 cm) or more.

Some experts believe a male chimp is
even more dangerous than a male lion.

One big meal is enough to keep some sharks alive
for many months.

Some prehistoric snakes were as long as a bus
and as heavy as a car.

The deadliest insects are microscopic
bugs, such as bacteria that cause serious sickness.

Wolves will attack bison, which are
more than 10 times larger than them.

Sharks lose thousands of teeth over a lifetime, but new
ones replace them.

Horned lizards defend themselves by squirting
blood from their eyes.

There are an estimated 10,000,000,000,000,000 ants in the world, and most of them can bite or sting!

A killer whale hits seals with its head or thumps them with its tail to kill them.

There are nearly 400 different types of shark, but only about 12 of them are dangerous to humans.

Some crocodiles can gallop, chasing their prey at up to 11 miles (17 km) per hour.

Bird-eating spiders shoot stinging hairs at their victims, causing intense pain.

A polar bear can kill an adult walrus that is more than twice its size.

The smallest shark in the world, the dwarf lanternshark, grows to just 7.8 in. (20 cm) long.

About 2.5 million people are bitten by snakes every year.

Funnel-web spider venom is deadly to humans and monkeys, but not to most other animals.

Wolverines often steal the kills of smaller predators such as foxes.

TAKING IT FURTHER

What makes a creature "scary"? Now it's time for you to decide.

- Choose some scary features, such as speed, size, weapons (such as teeth, claws, or jaws), aggressive personality, favorite food, and special powers (such as venom or camouflage).

- Use this book, and the Internet, to award up to five points for each of the animal's scary features. Repeat for as many animals as you want.

- Turn your results into a table, graph or chart. Add up the totals to get a "Scary Score" for each deadly creature.

USEFUL WEBSITES

www.sharktrust.org
Discover more about the interesting world of sharks.

www.flmnh.ufl.edu/fish/sharks
A great website for finding up-to-date information on sharks.

ocean.nationalgeographic.com/ocean
For facts and photos about sharks and their habitat.

crocodilian.com
Plenty of information on crocodiles, alligators and caimans.

www.reptilegardens.com
An introduction to reptiles of all types and sizes.

www.sciencedaily.com
For the latest exciting news on science from around the world.

venomous-spiders.nanders. dk/spiderpictures.htm
Research lots more deadly spiders, in creepy close-up.

www.zsl.org/kids
Enjoy animal games, books and funny facts.

www.biology4kids.com/files/invert_ main.html
Discover more invertebrates at this fact-packed website.

kids.nationalgeographic.com/kids
A great site for exploring the natural world.

www.kidsbiology.com
This website has a database of hundreds of animals.

www.bigcats.com
Play games and see amazing photos of big cats.

www.bears.org
Are all bears deadly? You can find out here.

gowild.wwf.org.uk
The World Wildlife Fund looks after animals and their homes.

www.arkive.org
Essential information on endangered animals.

GLOSSARY

alpha pair
A male and female pair that are the dominant animals in a group such as a pack of wolves.

ambush
A surprise attack made by an animal that has been lying hidden from view.

antivenom
A medicine that destroys deadly venom in a person's body.

bacteria
Tiny life forms that are too small to see with the naked eye. Bacteria are found wherever there is life on Earth.

basking
Lying in a warm place, such as sunlight, in order to get warm.

beaching
When a sea animal, such as a whale, becomes stranded on land.

binocular
Seeing using both eyes together. Binocular vision is good for hunting.

camouflage
A pattern of colors on an animal's body that hides it from predators or prey.

cannibals
Animals that eat others from the same species.

capybara
A large rodent that lives in the grasslands of South America.

cartilage
A strong, flexible fiber in animals' bodies. Sharks' skeletons are made from cartilage.

clotting
The process by which blood thickens after a wound has been made.

colony
A large group of animals living closely together.

constrictor
A kind of snake that kills its prey by squeezing it to death.

courtship
A series of rituals, such as flying displays, that animals perform to select a mate.

denticles
Hard scales on a shark's skin that help it to swim faster.

extinct
A species of animal that is no longer alive.

fangs
Long, pointed teeth that animals use for biting and tearing flesh.

freshwater
Water without salt in it, such as that found in lakes and rivers.

gills
Organs used by fish to breathe. The gills collect oxygen that is dissolved in the water.

girth
The distance around a body. The thicker its body, the bigger its girth.

gorge
To eat a huge amount of food at one time.

hosts
Animals that parasites such as mosquitoes feed on.

hatch
The breaking out of a baby animal from its egg.

invertebrates
Animals such as insects and spiders that do not have a backbone.

larvae
The young of animals such as insects, which change shape completely when they become adults.

marsupial
A kind of mammal, such as a kangaroo or a Tasmanian devil, that gives birth to very small young, which grow in a protective pouch in their mother's body.

mating
When a male and a female animal come together to reproduce.

nervous system
A network of nerve cells in an animal's body that carries signals to and from the brain.

paralyze
To stop a part of an animal's body from moving or feeling pain.

parasites
Animals or plants that feed on other animals or plants, called hosts. Parasites often cause their hosts harm.

plankton
Small animals and plants that float in the oceans, carried along by the ocean currents.

predators
Animals that hunt other animals to eat.

prey
Animals that are hunted by predators.

pup
The young of a shark.

radar
A system that uses radio waves to detect objects. The system gives off radio waves, then senses any waves that bounce back off objects in their way.

saliva
A liquid made inside an animal's mouth.

scavenger
An animal that feeds on dead animals or plants that it finds. Some sharks are scavengers.

segments
Parts of an animal's body that are similar to each other.

sensors
Organs in an animal that respond to stimuli such as light or magnetism.

serrations
A series of sharp points that make a sawlike cutting edge.

shed
To take off the outer layer of skin. Snakes shed their skin as they grow.

solitary
Living alone, away from other members of the same species.

species
A kind of animal or plant. Members of the same species are able to breed, producing young.

stalking
A method of hunting in which a predator follows its prey very quietly. When it gets up close to the prey, it attacks.

stealth
Moving carefully and quietly in order to sneak up on prey.

streamlined
A smooth shape that allows fluids such as water to flow easily around it.

stun
To knock an animal out suddenly.

suffocate
To die due to lack of oxygen, caused by not being able to breathe.

talons
The sharp claws of birds of prey.

tame
Not afraid of friendly humans.

toxins
Poisonous substances made in the bodies of some animals, which the animals use to attack other animals.

venom
A harmful substance that an animal injects into its victim's body by biting or stinging.

INDEX